His Mighty
WARRIORS

This book is presented to:

Tyler and Trenton

Love,

Grammie + Papa

Landuina

His Mighty
WARRIOR

Treasured Letters from Your King

Sheri Rose SHEPHERD

Illustrations by Lisa Marie Browning

MULTNOMAH
BOOKS

HIS MIGHTY WARRIOR
PUBLISHED BY MULTNOMAH BOOKS
12265 Oracle Boulevard, Suite 200
Colorado Springs, CO 80921
A division of Random House Inc.

ISBN 978-1-60142-034-3

Cover and interior design by Robin Black.

Library of Congress Cataloging-in-Publication Data
Shepherd, Sheri Rose, 1961–
    His mighty warrior : treasured letters from your King / Sheri Rose Shepherd ; illustrations by Lisa Marie Browning.— 1st ed.
        p. cm.
    ISBN: 978-1-60142-034-3
    1. Boys—Prayers and devotions. I. Browning, Lisa. II. Title.
    BV4855.S54 2007
    242'.62—dc22

                                    2007028091

Printed in the United States of America
2007—First Edition

10 9 8 7 6 5 4 3 2 1

I want to dedicate this book to all the young warriors
who will one day become great men of God.
I pray you discover your true identity in Christ,
fight the good fight, and become a hero of the faith.
May our God keep you safe as you grow and
prepare you for awesome adventures with the King!
I also want to specially dedicate this book
to God's mighty warriors:
Jake Jeppsen, Tucker Flannery,
Connor Barham, Garrett Ruiz,
Nathaniel, Harrison, and Jackson Ray,
Jefferson and Dexter Tuten,
and Ryan Funk.
Be strong in the Lord!

SHERI ROSE SHEPHERD

LETTERS FROM THE KING

His Mighty
WARRIOR

CHOSEN BY THE KING

My Son,

I have chosen you to do something great for my kingdom. You are not just a boy—you are a child of the King, and I am your Father in heaven. I want you to know that I am the same God who chose King David when he was just a little boy, and I have chosen you to show the world who I am. I will give you all you will ever need to conquer and accomplish the mission I have for you. Never forget who you are or who I am, and you will become a strong and mighty warrior for me.

Love,

Your King and Father in heaven

For you are a people holy to the LORD your God.
The LORD your God has chosen you out of all the peoples on
the face of the earth to be his people, his treasured possession.

DEUTERONOMY 7:6

Dear God,

Help me remember that you chose me and I am yours.

Please use each day of my life to prepare me to be

great in your kingdom. Thank you

for picking me out to be a warrior for you!

In Jesus's name I pray, amen.

A PLAN AND A PURPOSE

My Mighty Warrior,

I have a powerful plan for you, my son. I know you are just a young boy, but so was King David when I chose him to become the future king. Little did he know, while he was faithfully protecting and caring for sheep, that I was preparing him to protect and care for my people one day. Right now I have placed people in your life and given you special jobs to prepare you for your purpose in life. Be faithful in the little things and I will make you great in my kingdom.

Love,

Your King, who has a plan for you

~∾⌇∽~

"For I know the plans I have for you,"
declares the LORD, "plans to prosper you
and not to harm you, plans
to give you hope and a future."

JEREMIAH 29:11

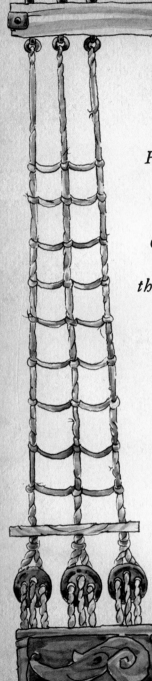

Dear God,

Help me to work hard and be faithful

at all the things you give me to do.

Give me a heart that wants to do the

things you planned out for me long ago.

I know I'm still young,

but I am mighty because of you!

In Jesus's name I pray, amen.

REAL HEROES...RESCUE

My Son,

You were born to be a hero, not to show off or use your strength to push others around. You are destined to rescue those who are hurting, to help those who are in need. I gave you my Holy Spirit when you invited me into your heart, and I have blessed you with spiritual eyesight to see people's hearts and hurts. If you ask me, I will empower you with a supernatural ability to do great things during your lifetime. Remember, you can do nothing apart from me. So come to me for your daily assignments and watch me make you into the hero you want to become.

Love,

Your Father in heaven and your strength

I have fought the good fight,
I have finished the race,
I have kept the faith.
2 TIMOTHY 4:7

6

Dear God,

Please forgive me when I do not help others when they are hurting. I do want to become a hero who helps all the people I can. I pray you will make me into a real hero of faith for you and your kingdom.

In Jesus's name I pray, amen.

POWER UP WITH PRAYER

My Warrior,

Because you are my son, I have given you special access to my throne room. I want you to power up every day with prayer. I want you to know that I, the God who created heaven and earth, can hear every word you say to me and that I love when you come to me. Remember, you can come to me about anything, anytime, because you are my son. I am never too busy to spend time with you. As you pray and enter into my presence, you will feel me strengthen you more and more. Come to me every day, my son, and I will take you on awesome adventures beyond what you could ever imagine.

Love,

Your Father, who is waiting to hear from you

Then Samson called to the LORD, saying,
"O Lord GOD, remember me, I pray!
Strengthen me, I pray, just this once,
O God, that I may with one blow take
vengeance on the Philistines for my two eyes!"

JUDGES 16:28, NKJV

Dear God,

I know I cannot do supernatural things

in my own strength, so help me remember

to power up with prayer. Help me

never be afraid to tell you everything.

Help me know you are always there.

In Jesus's name I pray, amen.

CHARACTER COUNTS

My Son,

I want you to be a guy with great character. Character is how you act when no one is watching. It is doing the right thing when you do not want to. Character is what really counts if you want to be a true spiritual hero. Anyone can look like they are doing the right thing when people are watching. But I want you to show me that you will do whatever I ask—when no one sees you but me. This may be hard, but I will help you when you are weak. I will place you in high places when you grow up if you will obey what I ask you to do now while you are young.

Love,

Your King and your strength to do the right thing

A good name is more desirable than great riches; to be esteemed is better than silver or gold.
PROVERBS 22:1

Dear God,

Forgive me when I choose not to do

the right thing. Sometimes it's hard

to do the right thing when I don't feel like it.

So please help me become a young man of

character who sets a good example

for others to follow.

In Jesus's name, amen.

THE POWER OF A PROMISE

My Strong Warrior,

A promise is a powerful thing. I want you to know that I, your Father in heaven, will never break a promise to you. As my warrior, I want you to keep your promises to others. It is very important that you do whatever it is you say you will do so that people will trust you. Think about how you feel when someone breaks a promise to you: it hurts, and it's hard to believe that person the next time they tell you they are going to do something. I want you to be careful when you make a promise, because broken promises cause broken hearts and you are called to rescue those who are hurting. If you keep your promises, you will be blessed by me and respected by others.

Love,

God, who always keeps his promises to you

Above all, my brothers, do not swear—not by heaven or by earth or by anything else. Let your "Yes" be yes, and your "No," no, or you will be condemned.

JAMES 5:12

12

Dear God,

Forgive me for the times I have broken my promises.

Help me remember how powerful my promises are.

Help me to do what I say I will do, because

I represent you. Thank you that you always keep

your promises to me.

In your name I pray, amen.

CONTAGIOUS COURAGE

My Brave Boy,

I will give you great courage, like I gave to King David, when as a young boy he fought a giant. Courage will not be easy, but it will help you remain strong when others around you are weak. As you grow, you will find there will be many times when you will be tempted to cave in to peer pressure. Remember this: anyone can follow a crowd or be a coward, but you have been appointed by me to stand and be courageous. I will be with you in the tough times, so call out to me in faith. I will give you the courage and strength to fight anyone or anything that comes against you.

Love,

Your God, who will give you strength

Be strong and courageous. Do not be afraid or terrified because of them, for the LORD your God goes with you; he will never leave you nor forsake you.

DEUTERONOMY 31:6

Dear God,

I need you. I cannot have courage without you.

Please give me the spirit of courage,

and give me the strength to be strong

and mighty for your kingdom.

Thank you that I do not have

to walk through tough times alone.

In Jesus's name I pray, amen.

PROTECTOR
OF THE KINGDOM

My Son,

I want to train you to protect those you love.
First, you need to stay alert and look for things
that might endanger your family or friends. When
you see trouble lurking in your territory, put up a
shield of protection first by praying. Next, sound the
alarm by using your words to send a warning. Last,
do what I ask you to do in my Word.
Then you will become the
protector I have prepared you
to be.

Love,

Your King, who is
   always alert

16

Be strong and very courageous. Be careful to obey all the law
my servant Moses gave you; do not turn from it to the right or to
the left, that you may be successful wherever you go.

JOSHUA 1:7

Dear God,

Train me to become a great protector for those I love.

I want to be alert to the Enemy's evil plans,

and I want to stop those plans with your wisdom and

strength. So please show me how.

In Jesus's name I pray, amen.

DIVINE ASSIGNMENTS

My Mighty Warrior,

Life is an adventure when you walk with me. I want you to be powered up with prayer every morning so that you do not miss the secret assignments I have planned for you. Remember, anyone can do good things to feel good about himself. But you, my warrior, will do great things that will further my kingdom and save people from a life of destruction and doom. So pray for your divine assignment every day, and I, your Father in heaven, will make it happen in the perfect time and place, according to my plans.

Love,

Your King, the great adventurer

I will make you into
a great nation and I will bless you;
I will make your name great,
and you will be a blessing.
GENESIS 12:2

Dear God,

What an adventure it is to be a part of

your plan! Help me to see what you

have divinely planned for me to do while

I am here on earth. I love being

a warrior for you, God!

In Jesus's name I pray, amen.

A Tender Warrior

Mighty Young Man,

I have created you to fight the good fight of your faith. But to do a good job, you must learn to love people. Remember that I, your Father in heaven, am love. As my warrior, you must learn to be as kind as you are tough. You must be as gentle with others as I am with you. Then you will win the hearts of people, and they will want to follow you.

Love,

Your Father in heaven, who is love

Therefore, as God's chosen people,
holy and dearly loved, clothe yourselves with compassion,
kindness, humility, gentleness and patience.
COLOSSIANS 3:12

Dear God,

It is hard sometimes for me to act tender

and kind when I don't feel that way in my heart.

So please change my heart,

and make me into your tender warrior.

In Jesus's name I pray, amen.

POWERFUL WORDS

My Warrior,

I have given you a powerful weapon—your words. You can use your words to wound others, or you can ask me to give you words that make others feel special. If you wound someone with your words by accident or on purpose, I want you to go right away and fix it by saying you are sorry. If you choose to be a tender warrior with your words, I will give you some very special blessings. Remember, because you are mine, you must use your words to help, not hurt.

Love,

Your King, who will help you speak life

Wise words satisfy like a good meal;
the right words bring satisfaction.

PROVERBS 18:20, NLT

∽⤳

Dear God,

I want to use my words to make others feel special.

So please help me say things that help others,

not hurt them, and forgive me when I don't.

In Jesus's name I pray, amen.

Family Matters

Mighty Young Man of Mine,

I have made you part of my family, and I love you more than words can say. I have also given you a family on earth that I want you to love the way I love you. I know your family is not perfect. But neither are you, my son, and I love you anyway. I am asking you to help your family or whoever takes care of you whenever you get the chance. Make them as important to you as you are to me, because your loved ones need you.

Love,

Your Father in heaven, God

A friend is always loyal,
and a brother is born to help in time of need.
PROVERBS 17:17, NLT

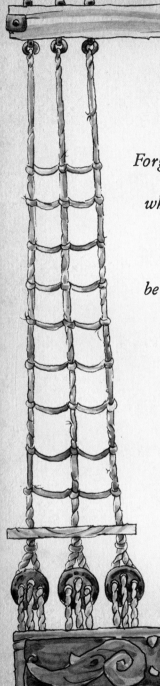

Dear God,

Forgive me for not always treating those

who take special care of me with love

and respect. Sometimes they can

be hard to love. I need you to help me

love them the way you love me.

I know I can only do this

with a heart like yours.

In Jesus's name I pray, amen.

RESPECT THE RULES

My Warrior,

You will be surrounded by boys and girls who do not want to follow the rules. I do not want you to be like them. I want you to be a leader, not a follower. A true leader will be strong and do the right thing. If you will do what I am asking of you, my son, I will do great things for you as you grow up. It is hard to respect rules when you do not understand them. But it is still the right thing to do, and it brings honor to me, your King.

Love,

Your Father, who will reward you

~❧~

Therefore, it is necessary to submit to the authorities, not only because of possible punishment but also because of conscience.

ROMANS 13:5

26

Dear God,

Please forgive me for the times I have not respected rules. Sometimes it is hard to follow rules, but I want you to be proud of me, so please help me obey the rules in my home and at my school.

In Jesus's name, amen.

CONQUER CONFLICT

My Warrior,

Sometimes your greatest fight will be with your friends or family. I want you to remember that no one is perfect and that people will say things that hurt you or make you mad. When this happens, I want you to come to me and pray. I will heal your heart if you ask me to, and I will give you the strength to forgive others. I know how hard it is to forgive those who have hurt you. But remember, my son, I always forgive you when you make mistakes. A warrior of mine does not let anyone stop him from being kind and strong in faith.

Love,

Your perfect King

If it is possible, as far as it depends on you,
live at peace with everyone.

ROMANS 12:18

❧

Dear Father in heaven,

Sometimes it is so hard to forgive

my friends and family when they hurt me.

So please help me,

because I can't do it on my own.

In Jesus's name, amen.

BE YOUR BEST

My Warrior,

I am so pleased when you do your best. I want you to try hard in everything you do, because you are not just an ordinary boy; you are mine. When you do your best—in school, at home, or in any sport or activity—others will see there is something special about you. Remember that whatever you do, I want you to do it for me, and I will bless you in a wonderful way.

Love,

Your King, who deserves your best

Work hard so you can present yourself to God and receive his approval. Be a good worker, one who does not need to be ashamed and who correctly explains the word of truth.

2 TIMOTHY 2:15, NLT

Dear God,

Please forgive me when I choose

not to do my best. Give me the desire

to be my best for you. Help me remember

that I represent you in all I do. And help me

to give my best and make you proud.

In Jesus's name I pray, amen.

HIDDEN TREASURES

My Warrior,

Don't miss out on all the treasures of truth hidden in the Bible. I have many amazing things in my Word that you will discover every time you read it. My Word will make you wise. It will give you the secrets to living a good life, and it will teach you how to become a strong and mighty warrior here on earth. Reading will help you know who I am and all I have for you, my son. So open your Bible every day, and discover all about your great faith adventure.

Love,

God, the giver of the Word

Do good to your servant, and I will live;
I will obey your word.
Open my eyes that I may see
wonderful things in your law.
PSALM 119:17–18

Dear God,

Thank you for your treasured Word.

I am so excited to discover all your secret wisdom!

Please help me when I read the Bible to understand
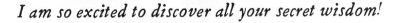

who you are and who I am.

In Jesus's name I pray, amen.

CHOOSE LIFE

My Chosen Warrior,

I want you to do all that I ask, but I will never force you to obey me. Just as I gave all of my children in the Bible a choice, I am also giving you a choice—the choice to live for me and my kingdom. I love you no matter what you do, my boy, but your life will be so much better if you choose to follow me and my way.

Love,

Your God, who gives life

❧

He predestined us to be adopted as his sons through Jesus Christ, in accordance with his pleasure and will.

EPHESIANS 1:5

Dear God,

Forgive me when I don't make good choices.

I need your help because I really do

want to follow you. I want to show you

how much I love you, Lord, by the

choices I make. Please help me.

In Jesus's name I pray, amen.

FIGHT THE GOOD FIGHT

My Mighty Warrior,

Sometimes life will get hard, but I have created you to fight the good fight of your faith. There will be many things and people who try to take away your faith in me. Do not listen to them; they are not of my kingdom. You will be a good defender of the faith if you obey me, know my Word, and pray.

Love,

Your Faith and Father in heaven

36

Be on your guard; stand firm in the faith;
be men of courage; be strong.

1 CORINTHIANS 16:13

❧

Dear God,

Help me fight the good fight

and never walk away from you.

I love you, and I want to always be your warrior.

In Jesus's name I pray, amen.

HONOR OTHERS

My Young Warrior,

I want to teach you how to honor others. *Honoring* is treating someone as very special and of high importance. There are many ways to honor people: stand when they enter a room, be a good listener, ask how you can help them. If you honor others, people will see that you are mine and you will become a young man of honor yourself.

It pleases me to see you treat others with honor.

Love,

Your King, who deserves your honor

Be devoted to one another in brotherly love.
Honor one another above yourselves.

ROMANS 12:10

Dear God,

Teach me to treat others with honor,

and help me know how

to become a young man of honor.

I know I honor you by honoring others.

In Jesus's name I pray, amen.

MONEY MATTERS

My Son,

I want to talk to you about money. Many
people have made money their god. That makes
me very sad, because they care more about money
than about me. I do not want you to be like that.
If you will put me first in your life, I will give
you the money and food you need to live.
Remember that no amount of money can buy a
home with me in heaven. What you do for my
kingdom is much more valuable than how much
money you have. So invest your time and talent in
helping others know me, and you will have a rich
life in your heavenly home.

Love,

Your God, who has riches
for you in heaven

Do not store up for yourselves treasures on earth,
where moth and rust destroy,
and where thieves break in and steal.

༽

Dear God,

I want to be really rich in heaven,

so please help me care more about your kingdom

than money here on earth. And use me

to do great things to further your kingdom.

In Jesus's name I pray, amen.

TAKE THE LEAD

My Son,

You, my great and mighty leader, were not meant to fit into the ways of this world. You were chosen by me to stand out. That means you cannot follow anyone who is making bad choices or you will get hurt. Remember my warning about this as you grow up and be the leader. I have appointed you to show others how to do the right thing and make good choices that please me. I will help you lead if you will ask me to in prayer.

Love,

Your leader who loves you, God

Know that the LORD has set apart the godly for himself;
the LORD will hear when I call to him.

PSALM 4:3

❧

Dear God,

I want to grow up to be a great leader.

Help me make the kind of choices that

will help others see that I am yours.

I also pray for our leaders in this country.

Help them, God, to do a good job.

In Jesus's name I pray, amen.

A MOTHER'S LOVE

My Boy,

I have given you a mother just as I gave my Son, Jesus, his mother, Mary. I want you to honor and respect your mother, no matter how your friends treat their mothers. Your mother is a gift from me. She will teach you how to be tender and loving, so treat her special, and tell her I love her too.

Love,

Your God and Father in heaven

My son, obey your father's commands,
and don't neglect your mother's instruction.

PROVERBS 6:20, NLT

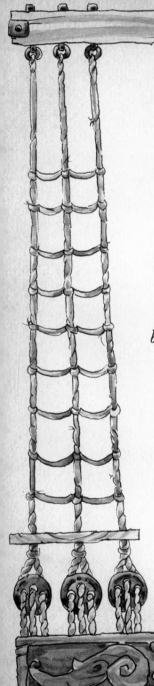

Dear God,

Please forgive me for the times

I have not treated my mom nicely.

Help my mom to raise me,

and help me to treat her special

by honoring and respecting her even

when I do not feel like it.

In Jesus's name I pray, amen.

DEALING WITH DISAPPOINTMENT

My Strong Boy,

Life will not always go the way you want it to. People will disappoint you, and it will hurt. First, I want you to know I am here whenever you are dealing with disappointment. I myself get hurt when my children turn from me. I love you, and I will help you no matter how hard things might seem. I am in control, and in tough times, I will teach you great things that will help you become great. So do not look to people; look to me.

Love,

Your God, who is always here

∽◎◈

*Trust in the LORD with all your heart
and lean not on your own understanding.*

PROVERBS 3:5

Dear God,

I need you to help me when things

do not go the way I want or when friends

or family disappoint me. Help me remember

that you will never leave me.

In Jesus's name I pray, amen.

When Anger Happens

My Young Warrior,

There will be many times that you will feel angry. I understand your anger, and I am not mad at you for feeling that way. I am asking you not to do things when you are mad, because you might hurt others and yourself. King David always cried out to me in his anger, and I answered. I want you to be like King David. Call out to me when you are angry, and I will help change your heart and help you through your anger.

Love,

Your God, who is slow to get angry

In your anger do not sin;
when you are on your beds,
search your hearts and be silent.

PSALM 4:4

Dear God,

Thank you for not getting mad at me for how I feel. I like having a Father in heaven who understands my heart. When I feel angry help me to still do the right thing. In Jesus's name I pray, amen.

NEVER ENOUGH

My Mighty Young Man,

I want to warn you about something that could make you unhappy no matter what you have. It is something that makes people do bad things. It is called greed. Greed is when you always want more. People who are greedy are never happy, and sometimes they will steal things or hurt others to get more. I want you to be happy with whatever you have. I will give you what you need and more, because I love when your heart is grateful for what you have now.

Love,

God, the giver of gifts

Every good and perfect gift is from above, coming down from the Father of the heavenly lights, who does not change like shifting shadows.

JAMES 1:17

Dear God,

I want to confess that sometimes I am

not grateful for what I have

and I feel greedy. Please help me

to enjoy what I have, and help me

find joy in giving to others also.

In Jesus's name I pray, amen.

TELL THE TRUTH

My Superhero,

Sometimes it is hard to tell the truth, especially if you will get punished for something you did wrong. All my children are tempted to lie, and sometimes lying looks easier, but truth is an important part of becoming a mighty warrior. If you lie, others will not trust you. And I do not reward lies, my son. I will give you the courage to tell the truth, if you will ask me. I will also bless you with a clean and happy heart for being honest with me and others.

Love,

God, who always tells the truth

There is no truth in [the devil].
When he lies, he speaks his native language,
for he is a liar and the father of lies.

JOHN 8:44

Dear God,

Please forgive me for the times I have lied. Help me

have the courage to tell the truth even if I will be

punished for something I did wrong. Please help me tell

the truth first so I will bring honor to you.

In Jesus's name I pray, amen.

TEACHERS RULE

My Mighty Warrior,

You have a lot to learn if you are going to become great in my kingdom. I have given you teachers to help you become smart and wise. I want you to listen to their instructions and treat them with honor. Teachers are a gift from me, and they are a gift to you as well. Learn all you can while you are young so that when you are grown, you will be a good leader.

Love,

Your God and teacher of life

He said to them, "Therefore every teacher of the law who has been instructed about the kingdom of heaven is like the owner of a house who brings out of his storeroom new treasures as well as old."

MATTHEW 13:52

Dear God,

Thank you for my teachers.

Help me learn all you want me to learn

and to treat my teachers with respect

even when I do not agree with everything

they do. I know this pleases you.

In Jesus's name I pray, amen.

SUPER SERVER

My Warrior,

I sent my Son, Jesus, to show you how to serve others. Because you are mine, I want you to serve others just as Jesus did while he was on earth. I want you to ask your family or friends how you can help them and look for ways to help anyone you can. When you do this, you will become great in my kingdom and your heart will be filled with joy.

Love,

Your God, who serves you

For even the Son of Man did not come
to be served, but to serve,
and to give his life as a ransom for many.

MARK 10:45

⁓ೋ⌀

Dear God,

Give me a heart like Jesus's.

Help me to think about others and to

serve them like a superhero serves his city.

In Jesus's name I pray, amen.

LOVE YOUR FAMILY

My Mighty Warrior,

I want you to be mighty in loving your family. They need you to love them as much as you need them to love you. I want you to love them with more than words, my son. Express your love with your actions also. I know sometimes it is hard to love family members when they are hurtful or tease you. So when it gets hard to love, remember that no matter how you act or what you do, I still love you.

Please know that I am always here to help you become a tender warrior who knows how to express love.

Love,

Your God, who is love

Go home to your family and tell them how much the Lord has done for you and how good he has been to you.

MARK 5:19, CEV

Dear God,

Help me love my family the way you love me.

It is hard sometimes, but I really want to

learn to love them. Forgive me for

the times I have said or done things to

hurt them or make them feel unloved by me.

In Jesus's name I pray, amen.

59

An Awesome Attitude

My Mighty Warrior,

I want to share with you another secret about becoming a great leader. All heroes of mine make a choice to have great attitudes no matter what happens. I want you to have the kind of attitude that shows others you are mine. Many people around you will have bad attitudes, but I do not want you to be like them. *Remember, no one can steal your joy unless you allow them to.* So learn to dig deep, just as you would dig for a treasure, to find a reason to be grateful. Then you will discover that a good attitude is more valuable than any amount of money or gold.

Love,

Your God, who is grateful for you

Be joyful in hope, patient in affliction,
faithful in prayer.

ROMANS 12:12

~⊙~

Dear God,

I want an awesome attitude.

Please help me have a grateful heart no matter

what happens. I want to be a hero for you

and help others do the same by my example.

In Jesus's name I pray, amen.

Bragging and Boasting

My Mighty Warrior,

I, your God, have given you special talents that others do not have. I will use you to do great things for me and my kingdom. But I do not want you to brag or make others feel bad for what they do not have or cannot do. You have been chosen by me to help others feel good about who they are and how I created them as well. So be careful, my boy, not to brag about the blessings I will give you throughout your life.

Love,

Your God, who is proud of you

Dear God,

Thank you for the way you made me, Lord.

Please teach me to help others feel good about

how you created them also. I am sorry for the times

I have bragged and made others feel bad.

In Jesus's name I pray, amen.

Run Your Own Race

My Warrior,

I have set before you a great race to run, and I want you to finish strong for me. To win this race you will need to keep your eyes on me, your Father in heaven. Do not compare yourself or look to anyone else, or you will get tired of running. I will help you win the race of your faith, and I will help you win people for my kingdom. And when you are tired I will carry you to the finish line, because I love you.

Love,

Your God and coach for life

Do you not know that in a race all the runners run,
but only one gets the prize?
Run in such a way as to get the prize.

1 Corinthians 9:24

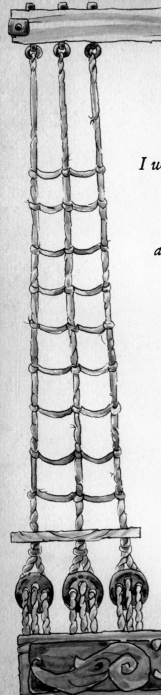

Dear God,

I want to be a strong runner in the race

of my faith. Help me look to you

and no one else so that I can finish

a winner for your kingdom.

In Jesus's name I pray, amen.

COME CLEAN

My Son,

I want you to know that nothing you do or say will ever stop me from loving you. But there is something that will make you feel separated from me. It is when you do something wrong and you do not tell me about it. I want you to come to me and confess when you know you have made a bad choice, and I will take away your shame and make you feel clean from the inside out. I will never make you feel bad for telling me your sins, and I will always forgive you.

Love,

Your King, who is quick to forgive

The LORD is compassionate and gracious,
slow to anger, abounding in love.

PSALM 103:8

66

Dear God,

I want to come to you now and say

I am sorry for when I do things that are wrong.

I thank you that you are a forgiving Father

and that I can confess anything to you.

In Jesus's name I pray, amen.

FEAR FACTOR

My Brave Warrior,

I have given you the spirit of courage, but there will be times that you may feel afraid or fearful. I want you to know that I am just a prayer away and that if you will call out to me, I will replace your fear with faith. You will feel my presence of peace every time you pray. So do not let the fear of anything stop you from coming to your Father in heaven. I will protect you as I protected all my Bible heroes throughout time.

Love,

Your God and protector

God will command his angels
to protect you wherever you go.
PSALM 91:11, CEV

Dear God,

Help me not to be afraid.

Remind me that you are always with me

and that I can trust you to protect me.

In Jesus's name I pray, amen.

WE ALL FALL DOWN

My Strong Warrior,

I love it when you stand strong and mighty and do the right thing, but I want you to know that I love you even when you do not. All of my children in the Bible made mistakes, and I was always there to pick them up when they fell. I do not expect you to be perfect, but I do expect you to let me help you get up and do the right thing when you fall.

Love,

Your God, who will always catch you when you fall

Even if good people fall seven times,
they will get back up. But when
trouble strikes the wicked,
that's the end of them.
PROVERBS 24:16, CEV

Dear God,

I am so glad I have a God who loves me no matter what. I know I make mistakes because I am not perfect, but thank you for loving me anyway. In Jesus's name I pray, amen.

A FAITHFUL FATHER

My Son,

I want you to know that I am your faithful Father. I will never leave you. I will be here for you always. You can come to me for anything you need. When you are hurting, I will soothe your pain. When you are excited about something, I will share in your pleasure. And when you need to talk, I am never too busy to listen. I am your faithful Father in heaven, who is with you wherever you go.

Love,

Your God and Daddy in heaven

Because you are sons, God sent the Spirit of his Son into our hearts, the Spirit who calls out, "Abba Father."

GALATIANS 4:6

Dear heavenly Father,

You are so great, and I am so thankful to be your son.

Thank you for adopting me into your family. I love

knowing that I am the son of the King of kings

and that I have a Father who is always there for me.

In Jesus's name I pray, amen.

A GREAT GIVER

My Warrior,

I am the giver of all good things. I love to give to my children. Because you are mine, I want you to have a heart that wants to share what you have and give to further my kingdom. If you see someone who is hungry, share your food. If you see a child without toys, give some of yours. You will become a hero who comes to the rescue if you learn to give, and then all will see that you are mine because you share all that you have. You will discover a great secret to a happy life…the more you give, the more I will give to you.

Love,

Your generous King

All they asked was that we should continue to remember the poor, the very thing I was eager to do.

GALATIANS 2:10

Dear God,

I want to become a great giver.

I want others to know that I give because

I love you. Please help me see with

supervision from you how

I can help others and give to anyone

who needs something I have.

In Jesus's name I pray, amen.

WALK AWAY
FROM THE WICKED

My Child,

I want to warn you about wicked people,
who are not a part of my kingdom. Because I
love you and I want to protect you from harm,
I have picked you to be a leader and a light in this
dark world. So I want you to walk away from people
who want you to disobey me. I will always make a way
for you to do the right thing. All you
have to do is ask me and I will
rescue you. Be strong, my son.
Walk away from the
wicked and become a
hero of the faith.

Love,

Your God and
protector

God blesses those people who refuse evil advice
and won't follow sinners or join in sneering at God.

PSALM 1:1, CEV

∼⦿∽

Dear God,

Help me walk away from anyone who wants

me to make bad choices, and help me always want to

follow you. When I walk in the wrong direction,

please turn me around and help me run to you instead.

In Jesus's name I pray, amen.

LOVE YOUR ENEMIES

My Mighty Warrior,

One of the hardest things I will ask you to do as my warrior is to pray for anyone who hurts you. I understand how hard it is to love a cruel person. But if you pray, I will give you the kind of heart you need to love your enemies. Remember, my boy, a warrior wants what is best for everyone. Even I, your Father in heaven, love those who sin against me and do not love me. This is my way and my will.

Love,

Your God and your strength

For God so loved the world that he gave his one and only Son, that whoever believes in him shall not perish but have eternal life."

JOHN 3:16

Dear Father in heaven,

It is really hard to love mean people.

I need you to help me. Remind me to pray for

them, and help me not to act like them.

In Jesus's name I pray, amen.

REVENGE IS MINE

My Mighty Warrior,

I want you to fight for what is right and be a strong warrior for my kingdom. But when others hurt you or anyone you love, I want you to let me repay their bad actions. I am a fair God, and no matter how bad things look, I promise that those who hurt my children will be punished by me in time. You can trust me. I want you to keep doing the right thing and to be the young man of faith I called you to be.

Love,

Your fair and just God

It is mine to avenge; I will repay.
DEUTERONOMY 32:35

Dear Lord,

I thank you that you will repay those cruel people

who hurt others, and I thank you that I do not

have to become like them. I trust you

in all things, and I hand them over to you,

my faithful Father who loves me.

In Jesus's name I pray, amen.

USE YOUR SHIELD

My Warrior,

I want you to be very careful what you watch on TV and what you read. Your eyes and mind play important roles in becoming a strong and mighty warrior. If you watch and read things that are not pleasing to me, you will become weak in your faith. So as your Father in heaven, I am asking you to put a shield over your eyes and turn your head when you see things that may weaken you, because you are called to be a strong warrior of mine.

Love,

Your God and your shield

Put on all the armor that God gives, so you can
defend yourself against the devil's tricks.

EPHESIANS 6:11, CEV

Dear God,

Open my eyes to see things that are not right

for a warrior to watch and read,

and help me guard my mind. Forgive me when I

give in to the temptation to put bad things in my mind.

In Jesus's name I pray, amen.

LOVE LIKE A HERO

My Son,

I want to give you supernatural eyesight to see people the way I do. Even though others are different from you, remember that I made each person on earth very special and very different, and I love what I have created. Because you represent me, I want you to treat everyone the same, whether they are rich or poor, old or young, black or white. If you will do this for your Father in heaven, you will become the kind of hero I created you to be and you will help others love one another by watching your example.

Love,

Your God, who loves you deeply

For everything we know about God's Word is summed up in a single sentence: Love others as you love yourself.

GALATIANS 5:14, MSG

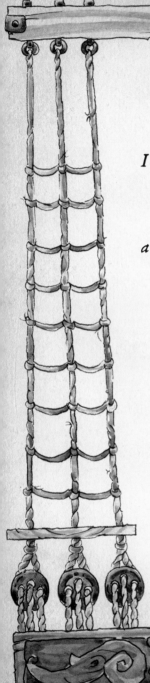

Dear God,

I want you to help me not to be selfish

with my friends. Help me be

a good friend to everyone around me.

In Jesus's name I pray, amen.

OBEY YOUR PARENTS

My Mighty Warrior,

I want you to obey your parents. I gave them to you to watch over you until you are grown. I know sometimes your parents are not perfect, but neither are you, my son. I will give you a good life if you will listen to them and obey them while you are young. It pleases your Father in heaven when you are kind and respectful and do what your parents ask you to do. I will give you a good, long life if you will honor and obey your parents.

Love,

Your God, who will bless you

❦

Children, obey your parents in the Lord,
for this is right. "Honor your father and mother"—
which is the first commandment with a promise—"that it may go
well with you and that you may enjoy long life on the earth."
EPHESIANS 6:1–3

Dear God,

Please give my parents wisdom on how to raise me,

and even though they are not perfect, help me obey them

because I love you. I want to be blessed by you,

so I need your help to honor and obey my parents.

In Jesus's name I pray, amen.

I Am the Truth

My Warrior,

To become great in my kingdom, you will need to trust that every word I have written in the Bible is true. I never lie, my son, and I always keep my promises. Every time you read my Word, you will discover another treasure of truth. You will also learn that my ways are not your ways, but my ways are the ways that will lead you to all the great adventures I have for you. I am the same God who parted the Red Sea for Moses and the same God who saved Noah's family from the great Flood, and I am the God who is truth.

Love,

Your King, who keeps his promises

I have placed my rainbow in the clouds.
It is the sign of my covenant
with you and with all the earth.
GENESIS 9:13 (NLT)

Dear Father in heaven,

I love being the son of a powerful God

who keeps his promises. Thank you

that I can always trust you.

Thank you for keeping your promises.

Help me to be like you and

keep my promises too.

In Jesus's name I pray, amen.

YOUR TRUE IDENTITY

My Mighty Warrior,

You are from a royal family, the kind of family that is of the greatest kingdom of all, my kingdom. You're a true, powerful prince because I am the King of kings; you have a very important position in life. You, my son, represent heaven on earth; you have anytime access to my throne room every time you pray. You have the power inside of you to do supernatural things that will make the world a better place to live because of my Spirit in you. If you will believe you are who I say you are, you will do great things in your life that will last forever

Love,

Your King and Father in heaven, God

But you are...a royal priesthood.
1 PETER 2:9

Dear heavenly Father,

I love knowing that I am your son and that I am chosen by you, the King above all kings. Thank you so much for letting me into your royal family. I pray I will represent you well to the world around me.

In Jesus's name I pray, amen.

WHEN BAD THINGS HAPPEN

My Warrior,

I am sorry to say you will discover that bad things will happen while you are on earth, even to my children. It is not my will that my people get hurt. Sadly, selfish sin has caused many people to walk away from me and do evil things. This breaks my heart because so many people suffer on earth due to their bad choices to disobey me. It won't always be that way, my son. Someday when you are done with your assignment on earth, you will be with me in heaven, where there are no more cruel people or pain. Only good things happen in my kingdom.

Love,

Your good God

The LORD mocks the mockers
but is gracious to the humble.
The wise inherit honor,
but fools are put to shame!
PROVERBS 3:34–35, NLT

Dear God,

Sometimes it is really hard to see people make bad things happen. Please help those people run from evil and give their hearts and lives to you.

Help me to remember that all bad things will end when you come back for us.

In Jesus's name I pray, amen.

HELP SAVE THE WORLD

My Mighty Warrior,

I have appointed you to be a strong superhero of faith in
this dark world. With my power you can help save people
from a life of destruction. I am the same God who gave
Moses the strength and words to set my people free. Just as
I helped Moses save my people from Pharaoh, I can help
you because my Spirit lives inside of you. Begin each day by
praying for my power and purpose for you, and watch me
perform miracles through you, my warrior.

Love,

Your God, who saved you

*The voice of the LORD called out to [Moses],
"I am the God of your ancestors—the God of Abraham, Isaac,
and Jacob." Moses shook with terror and did not dare to look.*

ACTS 7:31–32, NLT

Dear God,

I want to help build your kingdom.

I want to see people saved, so please give me

the words to say and the courage

to speak up and help save the world.

In Jesus's name I pray, amen.

REJECTION HAPPENS

My Son,

I want you to know that not everyone
will like you. Some people do not know how
to love or be loved. I also want you to know
that your Father in heaven was also rejected by
many people I created. I do not force people to love
me, and neither can you, my son. I want you to pray
for them. Those people cannot stop you from greatness
unless you let them. Remember, when
you feel rejected, that I will never
reject you.

Love,

Your God, who loves
   everything about you

Praise be to God, who has not rejected my prayer
or withheld his love from me!
PSALM 66:20

Dear God,

It hurts when people do not like me.

Help me love them and pray for them no matter

how they act. Help me not to act like that either.

In Jesus's name I pray, amen.

DEATH IS NOT THE END

My Mighty Warrior,

I never want you to be afraid of death, because death is not the end for those who belong to me. It is the beginning of forever life in heaven. When you or anyone who loves me leaves this earth, they get to be with me forever. In heaven no one is sick, no one is sad, and no one will ever die again. "Happily ever after" is a real thing in my kingdom. Anyone you love who comes to heaven before you will be here when you get here, and we will all be one big happy family forever.

Love,

Your God in heaven

Jesus told her, "I am the resurrection and the life. Anyone who believes in me will live, even after dying.
JOHN 11:25 (NLT)

Dear God,

Thank you for heaven. Please help me to remember when someone dies that they are with you and that I will see them again. And please comfort me when I miss them.

In Jesus's name I pray, amen.

REAL TREASURES
IN HEAVEN

My Royal Son,

One day you will live with me in heaven.
When you get here, I will have so many presents
and treasures to give you. Now, every time you do
something heroic, such as being kind, helping
someone, or telling someone about me, I add
another gift for your arrival. Remember this even if
no one notices the special things you do, my son.
I see everything, and I am so proud whenever you
show others that you are my tender warrior
through your acts of love and kindness. I cannot
wait to show you all the wonderful things I am
preparing for you.

Love,

Your God, who has great gifts to give

No eye has seen, no ear has heard,
and no mind has imagined what
God has prepared for those who love him.

1 CORINTHIANS 2:9, NLT

~~~

Dear God,

Thank you for all the great gifts you are preparing

for me. Help me do the mighty work you have for me

to do here on earth until that great day. I want

to be a hero in your eyes even if no one else notices.

In Jesus's name I pray, amen.

ABOUT THE AUTHOR

Sheri Rose is a woman who can relate to almost any woman's battle. This former Mrs. United States grew up in a dysfunctional home and was severely overweight as a teen. As a young woman, she battled depression and an eating disorder. She understands the pain that comes from a broken home, and she knows what it means to fight for freedom from your past. In spite of an English teacher telling her she was "born to lose" and a learning disorder—dyslexia—Sheri Rose has (in God's strength) written best-selling books and founded His Princess Ministries. She speaks to thousands each year at churches and women's conferences, and she had the 2006 number-one show of the year on Focus on the Family with Dr. James Dobson. For a free copy of that broadcast please visit www.hisprincess.com.

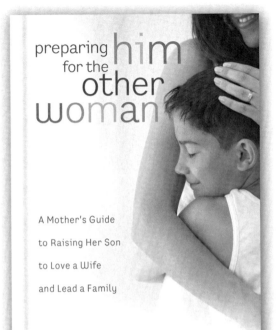

preparing him
for the other
woman

A Mother's Guide
to Raising Her Son
to Love a Wife
and Lead a Family

Sheri Rose Shepherd

What kind of husband will your son grow up to be?

Whether you're a single mom or married, you can raise a
son to love a wife and lead a family.

"I cannot think of a better way for a mother to invest her time than to prepare her son for the next first lady."
-Children's pastor, Kindred Community Church, Southern California

"Not only is this an amazing concept, but it meets an urgent need for every mother of boys."
-Lisa Bevere, Speaker and author of *Fight Like a Girl* and *Kissed the Girls and Made them Cry*

For more information, visit Sheri Rose's website at www.hisprincess.com

You Are God's Masterpiece

Give yourself the gift of hearing His voice speak directly to you in these beautiful scriptural love letters from your King. Let your soul soak in His love as each letter reminds you WHO you are, WHY you are here, and HOW much you are loved.

I have many devotional books, but very few have found their way into my morning quiet-time ritual. But from the first day I began His Princess *I knew this was a book I wanted to read every day. Encouraging and insightful, this book reminds me how special I am to my Lord. I love this book!*
— Tricia Goyer, author of *NeXt Generation Parenting*

For more information, visit Sheri Rose's website at www.hisprincess.com